1-2016

Celebrate Fall
Apples

Shores

CAPSTONE PRESS
a capstone imprint

Little Pebble is published by Capstone Press,
1710 Roe Crest Drive, North Mankato, Minnesota 56003
www.capstonepub.com

Library of Congress Cataloging-in-Publication Data
Shores, Erika L., 1976– author.
 Apples / by Erika L. Shores.
    pages cm.—(Little pebble. Celebrate fall)
 Summary: "Simple nonfiction text and full-color photographs present apples in fall"—Provided
by the publisher.
Audience: Ages 5–7
Audience: K to grade 3
Includes bibliographical references and index.
 ISBN 978-1-4914-6001-6 (library binding)—ISBN 978-1-4914-6013-9 (pbk.)—
 ISBN 978-1-4914-6025-2 (eBook pdf)
1. Apples—Juvenile literature. 2. Autumn—Juvenile literature. I. Title.
SB363.S545 2016
634.11—dc23   2015001839

Editorial Credits

Cynthia Della-Rovere, designer; Gina Kammer and Morgan Walters, media researchers;
Katy LaVigne, production specialist

Photo Credits

Alamy: Picture Partners, 21; Capstone Press: Gary Sundermeyer, 13; Capstone Studio: Karon
Dubke, 7, 9, 17; Dreamstime: Dave Bredeson, 19, Mahira, 16; iStockphoto: ericmichaud,
11; Shutterstock: Christian Jung, cover, Dancake, (dots in red line by photo) throughout,
Dionisvera, (ripe apple w/ leaf) throughout, Everything, (red apple) throughout, George
Dolgikh, 15, JIANG HONGYAN, (green apple) throughout, Jirapolphoto, (water on apples) 1,
2, 22, Maks Narodenko, (green apple w/ leaf) throughout, Mega Pixel, 12, Nitr, 5, pukach, 8,
Roman Samokhin, (red apple on side) throughout, SeDmi, 6

Printed in the United States of America
in North Mankato, Minnesota.
102015   009270R

Table of Contents

Apple Trees

Apples tell us fall is here!

Apple trees grow
in orchards.

Flowers on the trees are called blossoms. Blossoms fall off. Then apples grow.

apple

Picking Apples

Pick the ripe apples.
A basketful is called
a bushel.

Grab one to eat.

Take a great big bite!

The apple's center
is the core.
How many seeds
do you see?

I found six seeds
inside my apple!

Cut up
green apples.
Bake them in pies.

Time for a sweet

fall treat!

Glossary

blossom—a flower on a fruit tree

bushel—a way to measure an amount of apples

orchard—a field or farm where fruit trees are planted

ripe—ready to pick and eat

seed—the part that will grow into a new plant or tree

Read More

Griswold, Cliff. *Let's Go Apple Picking!* Fun in Fall. New York: Gareth Stevens Publishing, 2015.

Owen, Ruth. *Fruit!: Life on an Apple Farm.* Food from Farmers. New York: Windmill Books, 2012.

Smith, Sian. *What Can You See in Fall?* Seasons. Chicago: Capstone Heinemann Library, 2015.

Internet Sites

FactHound offers a safe, fun way to find Internet sites related to this book. All of the sites on FactHound have been researched by our staff.

Here's all you do:
Visit *www.facthound.com*
Type in this code: 9781491460016

Super-cool stuff! Check out projects, games and lots more at www.capstonekids.com

Index